WORLD'S COOLEST GRANDPA

Written by Lamar Golden

Illustrated by Alana McCarthy
www.AlanaMcCarthy.com

Masao Sawada is 78 years old and lives every day to the fullest.

He is retired and transitioned to be
Chairman of the Board for his own company.

He drives a cool car that is golden yellow.

He enjoys the wind blowing in his hair when he lets the top down.

He lives in a retirement home in Toyota City, Japan but takes trips often for fun.

Every morning at 6:00am
he wakes up.

Then he goes to breakfast
at 6:30am sharp.

After breakfast he takes a
walk to the convenience store.

He grabs his morning coffee,
talks to the store attendants,
and then walks back home.

Next, he plays sudoku for one hour while drinking his coffee.

Suddenly the phone rings and it's his granddaughter Liana.

Liana talks to GiGi for 1 hour while she eats her breakfast and GiGi listens carefully.

Liana tells GiGi goodbye and heads to school.

Masao replies: Goodbye and have fun at school.

Masao hangs up and drives to the grocery store to get some fresh fruit and vegetables.

Masao meets two people and has a conversation at the grocery store.

He pays for his groceries, puts them in his car and drives home.

Once he arrives home he unpacks the groceries and goes to the lounge in the senior home.

While in the lounge, he meets three friends having a conversation.

He joins the conversation, and they talk for one hour until 11:45am.

Masao says goodbye goes upstairs to get his golf clubs, then puts them in his car and drives to his favorite soba restaurant at 12:00pm.

After he eats he drives to the range and enjoys a game of golf.

He talks to some other golfers on the range and they decide to play together.

Masao finishes golfing at 5:30pm. He calls the best eel restaurant in town and makes a reservation for 6:30pm.

He gets in his car and drives 45 minutes across town to the eel restaurant and checks in.

The wait staff has him sit down in the lobby until his table is ready.

Once his table is ready, he gets seated and orders his food. The waitress brings hot tea and later returns 5 minutes with his eel and rice.

Masao eats his eel and rice and his granddaughter Liana video calls him and talks to him while he's eating.

Masao shows his granddaughter to the waitress while talking.

He finishes eating and says thank you afterwards and pays his bill.

He drives back home and brushes his teeth and takes a bath.

Then he goes to sleep.

The end.

This book was written to celebrate the life of Masao Sawada.

Thank you for being the example of how a man is supposed to be. I enjoy hanging out with you and learning from you.

Happy 78th Birthday and may you have many more.

Your son in law,

Lamar Golden.

Hardcover: ISBN: 978-1-960976-01-7

Paperback: ISBN: 978-1-960976-00-0

eBook: ISBN: 978-1-960976-02-4

Library of Congress Number: 2023907777

www.ingramcontent.com/pod-product-compliance
Lightning Source LLC
Chambersburg PA
CBHW041608120626
46551CB00002B/362